Cuttings

by

Ollie George Clark

Published by Playdead Press 2019

A CIP catalogue record for this book is available from the British Library.

ISBN 978-1-910067-79-6

Playdead Press
www.playdeadpress.com

Cuttings was first performed at The Hope Theatre, Islington, 4th June 2019 with the following company:

CAST

Ruchi	**Natasha Patel**
Gracelyn	**Joan Potter**
Danica	**Maisie Preston**

Featuring the voices of Elliot Liburd, Beth Organ & Dene Horgan

CREATIVE

Writer	**Ollie George Clark**
Producer	**Amy Hendry**
Director & Sound Design	**Rob Ellis**
Set & Costume Design	**Caitlin Abbott**
Lighting Design	**Holly Ellis**
Casting Associate	**Katharine Edmonds**
Stage Manager	**Gwenan Bain**

Thanks

My thanks must first go to Rob Ellis for his continued dedication to this script and enthusiasm to keep me driving towards the next draft. Equally, Dene Horgan for reading every countless draft and alteration, down to the full stops, and for that I'll be eternally grateful. To Tower Theatre, Dhanushuka Anson, Jamie-Rose Monk, Izzy Daws, Georgia Dacey and Theatre 503 for their support in allowing me to workshop the script and hear it aloud; and to the Hope Theatre for believing in the play.

Finally, thank you to all my friends, family and loved ones – it's for you that I continue to write.

Cover image: Cam Harle Photography | camharlephotography.com

The Hope Theatre is an award winning studio space in Islington, North London which opened its doors in 2013. It was the first Off West End venue to open with an in-house agreement with Equity, the UK's largest performers' union, to ensure a legal wage for all actors, stage managers and box office staff working at the theatre. The Hope Theatre is a place for audiences and companies to explore BIG ideas. It nurtures and develops new producing models, working with exciting companies to present a mix of new writing, lost gems from well-known writers, re-polished classics and innovatively staged musicals.

The Hope Theatre has won 5 Off West End Awards including Best Artistic Director for Matthew Parker in 2016 and was nominated as Fringe Theatre of the Year at the 2017 Stage Awards. The Hope Theatre has been home to over 30 world premieres and has seen many productions transfer to the West End and UK tours including *Ushers* to the Charing Cross Theatre, *46 Beacon* to the Trafalgar Studios and *Lovesong Of The Electric Bear* to The Arts.

The Hope Theatre
207 Upper Street
Islington
London
N1 1RL

www.thehopetheatre.com

Relish Theatre is a previously Norwich based theatre company dedicated to creating work that would appeal to a non-theatre going audience, and showcasing the work of regional talent.

Previous work

Time and Tide by James McDermott (Script Accelerator, Park Theatre, 2018)

Unicorn by Brad Johnson (Theatre N16, 2017),

A Matter Of Life And Debt by Samuel Masters (Edinburgh Fringe, 2015)

Relish Theatre are also producers of podcast *Theatre Feuds* and Theatre *Feuds Live!* (Theatre503, 2016)

Natasha Patel | Ruchi

Natasha is an Actress and Dancer with training at the Identity School of Acting, Unseen Drama School and Middlesex University.

Theatre includes *Lancastrians* (Junction 8 Theatre), *Remember / Jukebox* (Rifco Arts), *Mitridate Re Di Ponto* (Royal Opera House).

Film credits include *Aladdin* (Guy Ritchie), *A Grown Woman* (Delivery Film LTD), *Walking On Sunshine* (Vertigo Films). TV credits include *Doctor Who, Uncle* (BBC). Natasha has appeared in commercials for Levis, Special K, Smart Energy and Premier Inn.

Joan Potter | Gracelyn

Joan trained at Drama Studio London.

Theatre includes *Time And Tide* (Script Accelerator, Park Theatre), *The Lesson* (The Hope Theatre, 2018 OFFIE Nominated – Best Supporting Female), *The Balcony* (Bread and Roses Theatre), *The Tempest* (Bread and Roses Theatre; Etcetera Theatre; OSO Arts Centre), *The Taming Of The Shrew* (Etcetera Theatre; Cockpit Theatre), *A Midsummer Night's Dream, Macbeth, A Doll's House, The Positive Hour* (Grange Theatre).

Maisie Preston | Danica

Maisie graduated LAMDA in 2017.

Theatre includes *The Accidental Death of an Anarchist* (The OSO), *To See Ourselves* (Sliding Tackle Company) and *Little Echoes* (Hope Theatre).

She recorded the audio series *The Gnats* and filmed the Short Film *Wolf Among Sheep*.

Ollie George Clark | Writer

Ollie George Clark is a BAFTA Rocliffe Award Shortlisted writer from London. He trained on the Almeida Theatre Writing Group, and his Short Play, *Those We Exile* was produced for their Labyrinth Festival. Other work includes *Coconuts* (Lyric Hammersmith), *Warm And Chewy* (Old Red Lion), *The Strictly Curse* (Southwark Playhouse), *The Selfie Portrait* (Phoenix Arts Club), *Hold For Three Seconds* (Edinburgh Fringe). His feature length film *Asphodel* is being released in 2019, and his short film *Thoftly* is entering festivals in the summer.

Amy Hendry | Producer

Amy is a freelance Producer with a MA from the University of Kent.

Recent work includes the development of *Time and Tide* (Script Accelerator, Park Theatre) for Relish Theatre, *Shakespeare's Mad Women* (UK tour) for Lady Garden Theatre, of which she is also a co-founder. Currently an assistant at National Theatre Productions, she was production assistant on the West End transfer of *Nine Night*, and previously worked at the Michael Grandage Company (*School of Rock the Musical, Labour of Love, Red, The Lieutenant of Inishmore*). She was previously manager at both the Finborough Theatre, and New Diorama Theatre.

As a director/assistant director she has worked at The Marlowe Theatre, Canterbury, The Space, Isle of Dogs, Old Red Lion the Canterbury Shakespeare Festival, Theatre N16, Wise Words Festival, The Arts Theatre, and various productions at the Edinburgh Fringe.

Rob Ellis | Director & Sound Design

Rob has a Masters in Theatre Directing from the University of East Anglia.

Directing includes *The Merry Wives Of Windsor* (Théâtre de Verdure, Paris), *Time and Tide* (Script Accelerator, Park Theatre), *The Taming of the Shrew*, *The Two Gentlemen of Verona* (Quite Right Theatre), *Unicorn* (Theatre N16), *Bluebird* (Katzpace), *The 39 Steps* (Upstairs At The Gatehouse), *Six Pack* (Leicester Square Theatre), *Clybourne Park* (St Brides Institute), *A Matter Of Life and Debt*, *Positive* (Edinburgh Fringe).

As Associate / Assistant Diretor includes *Bismillah!* (UK Tour; Pleasance Theatre, Islington; VAULT Festival), *The Three Musketeers* (Iris Theatre, Covent Garden), *A Princess Undone* (Park Theatre), *The Passing Of The Third Floor Back* (Finborough Theatre).

Rob is the Artistic Director of Relish Theatre.

Caitlin Abbott | Set & Costume Design

Caitlin trained in Theatre Design at the Bristol Old Vic.

Set design includes *The Elephant Man* (Bristol Old Vic), *Tender Napalm* (The Wardrobe Theatre) *Airswimming* (Apprenticeship Showcase, Theatre Royal Haymarket) *Daughter of the Forest* (Richmix; UK Tour) *The Three Musketeers* (Pleasance Theatre, Tour), *Birangona* (UK & Bangladesh Tours), *The Jabberwocky* (Edinburgh Fringe), *Knitmas* (Greenwich Theatre Studio), *Bassett / Changing Room* (The Egg), *The Vikings at Helgeland* (Drayton Theatre), *The Winter's Tale* (Gdansk & Ostrava Shakespeare Festivals).

Costume Design includes *Pages of the Sea* (Weston Beach), *The Taming of the Shrew* (Circomedia).

She is currently Assistant Designer for the RSC.

Holly Ellis | Lighting Design

Holly trained at LAMDA.

She has worked on *The Rubinstein Kiss* (With Mike Robertson at Southwark Playhouse), *Half Me Half You* (Tristan Bates Theatre), *Lucy Light, LadyBones* and *Thomas* (Vaults Festival 2019), *Anomaly* (Old Red Lion), *Jeannie* (Finborough), *Sexy Laundry* (Tabard Theatre), *That Girl* (Old Red Lion), *Vanishing Man* and *Extinction* Event (High Tide and Pleasance Edinburgh 2018), *Sparks* (As Associate LD for Zoe Spurr, High Tide and Pleasance Edinburgh 2018), *Conquest* (Bunker), *War Plays* (Tristan Bates), *Cream Tea* and *Incest* (Hope Theatre), *Much Ado About Nothing, Twelfth Night, Comedy of Errors* (Karamel Club, Mountview). Please see her website at www.hollyellislighting.com

Katharine Edmonds | Casting Associate

Katharine graduated from Kent University in 2017, having studied Drama & Theatre with a year abroad at the University at Buffalo.

Previous work includes General Manager at Finborough Theatre and Associate Producer for Lady Garden Theatre Company. She is currently working as a casting assistant, predominantly on children's casting for theatre, including *Matilda* and *School of Rock*.

Gwenan Bain | Stage Management

Gwenan's work as a stage manager and operator includes *Little Echoes* (The Hope Theatre), *As We Unravel* (The Bread and Roses Theatre), *The Sword of Alex* (White Bear Theatre), *Metamorphoses 2* (Waterloo East Theatre) and a number of productions with Director's Cut Theatre (Gerry's Studio Stratford East; Southwark Playhouse).

In addition to her work in stage management, Gwenan was the Bread and Roses Theatre's emerging director for 2018, most recently directing *Other-Please Explain* for the Park Theatre's script accelerator program.

Other credits include *It Tastes Like Home* and *The Buzz* (assistant director, Bread and Roses Theatre), *Millennials* (Black Cat Theatre, The Pleasance) and Get Over It Productions' new writing night *The Scene* (Tabard Theatre).

This play is dedicated to my mother, father and brother for their unfaltering support.

CHARACTERS:

DANICA, around twenty three.

RUCHI, around twenty nine.

GRACELYN, around forty six.

OFF STAGE CHARACTERS:

ARTHUR MOSES, around twenty five.

ROXANNE REID, around forty six.

TELEVISION REPORTER, around thirty five.

SETTING:

The entirety of the play is set in contemporary London, in the head office of a Personal PR Agency.

(/) denotes a change of thought if in the middle of a line of dialogue, or an interruption if at the end.

Amongst all usual office items, left of stage sits a tidy, grand desk, with a potted plant on it and a large computer. Opposite are two chairs, one with a cushion. Right of stage is a large cupboard, locked, and next to it a glass door and a speedball.

At the back of the stage sits a tall, wide window and next to it a neon sign which reads: 'It's PR, not ER' next to which sits a television. Dangling from the ceiling, limply, hangs a clearly broken fire alarm.

Littering all the walls are framed pictures; some are movie posters, some theatre posters, some television, and the others are all of the same person: a middle-aged actress.

The phone is ringing continually, and shrilly, through the scene, unless said otherwise.

Enter DANICA. She turns on the lights and goes over and opens the window, and then clicks on the neon sign – it's a hideous red and it flickers into life – and turns on the computer, and then stares at the phone.

DANICA   (*calling out of the room*) It's on one hundred and twelve.

RUCHI   (*off stage, calling in*) What?

DANICA   A hundred and twelve, it's on one hundred and twelve missed calls.

The phone rings.

Christ.

Danica quickly presses a button.

One hundred and thirteen, but I handled it.

| RUCHI | Don't block them! Don't actually / just let them ring out. S'like we can't get to the phone. |
| DANICA | Oh, cool, 'kay. |

DANICA leans down and logs into the computer. The phone rings again, she watches patiently. It stops.

| | A hundred and fourteen and I'm learning. |
| RUCHI | Now you're getting it! |

DANICA moves to look at the walls and its pictures.

| DANICA | Ru? |

No answer.

	Ru!
RUCHI	Yeah?
DANICA	Did you say Jane or James?
RUCHI	When?
DANICA	Jane or James?

ENTER RUCHI, holding a plastic folder filled with the day's press cuttings, newspapers and a bag around her shoulder.

| RUCHI | James. Twelve o'clock, then Jane at three. |
| DANICA | Right. |

DANICA begins collecting the pictures of the actress, and taking them off the walls; RUCHI soon stops her, making her look at what she's holding and they sift through.

14

RUCHI   Look at him. Look at/ across the board. Fifteen of them. Front page or at least front page teasers from all.

DANICA   Nice pictures there.

RUCHI   The Sun have pissing led with it.

DANICA   So have The Times, is it a slow news day?

RUCHI   Well, no, not really, a bomb's gone off somewhere.

DANICA   Here, in The Times-

Reading from one of the articles.

'Former YouTube star turned actor, Arthur Moses' shockingly drink-fuelled swearing during the Olivier Awards last night stunned and repelled /

RUCHI   'Repelled' /

DANICA   'audience members, as well as those listening live on BBC Radio 4; ruining, what is for most, the highlight of the theatrical calendar'.

RUCHI snatches the paper.

RUCHI   Let me see.

Right-wing prudes. He only said cunt.

DANICA   Twice.

RUCHI   Well, he had to thank his agent and his manager.

DANICA   I'm not saying it's not apt, I'm saying he shouldn't have said it. And the only reason he said cunt was to mix things up from constantly saying fuck.

DANICA hands over the batch of cuttings, RUCHI takes them and places some on the desk; she then continues to cut out new cuttings from the unread papers. DANICA moves to the cupboard, unlocks it, takes out endless pictures of James' projects and puts them on the empty spaces on the wall.

RUCHI   It's a term of affection, he's from Stepney. We all need to calm ourselves. It's just a word.

DANICA   A word people don't like.

RUCHI   I think it's more who's saying it.

DANICA   Is this not all secretly good, though, in a strange way?

RUCHI shows the number of papers.

RUCHI   Not really, no.

DANICA   All this exposure?

RUCHI   Still no.

DANICA   'No such thing as bad publicity', isn't that the phrase?

RUCHI   There's actually no such a thing as good publicity, there's just planned and unplanned, and this is very much the latter.

DANICA   Well, press regardless, he looks like sex on legs in those photographs.

16

RUCHI　　That defence isn't strong enough for the national press. If it didn't work for Bieber, it's not going to work for Moses.

RUCHI takes the remaining cuttings, places them on the desk and sits on her phone.

DANICA　　So what is the defence?

RUCHI　　Standard twitter apology.

DANICA　　Saying? /

RUCHI　　Saying he's upset if you were offended; 'he hopes for forgiveness'; 'he's very embarrassed'; 'please accept his apology'; and then garnish with healthy doses of 'sorry'.

DANICA　　Could've been said by anyone.

RUCHI　　And is said by everyone. I've sent it to him for sign off but I've heard nothing back.

DANICA　　Was James in King Lear? The McKellen one at The Old Vic?

RUCHI　　No, didn't get it. We use Windermere's Fan, there, the Alien film and the dolphin puppet show.

DANICA　　Oh, yes! Right. So, just tweet the apology. Known each other long enough, haven't you?

RUCHI looks to her phone.

RUCHI　　It's not that easy, there's a sweet spot when it's print stories like this, how and when to respond. Too soon it's not him and he's guilty, too far and he's been forced. We need the ideal middle.

DANICA	Right.
RUCHI	Enough time for him to believably wake up, feel, understand and apologise of his own accord.
DANICA	So when's that then?
RUCHI	My thinking is 10. He'll wake up at 8 needing a wee, then go back to bed; get back up at 9 to rehydrate, glance at his phone, try to go back to sleep, but he won't settle so he'll reach for Twitter at 9.30; he'll then see the reactionary anger, panic, call his mum who'll direct him to us, we'll direct him to the draft and he'll tweet at 10 /
DANICA	That easy? /
RUCHI	Plus, that's when the arts journo's have staggered in and can update the story online.
DANICA	And in the meantime?
RUCHI	In the meantime, we buckle in and withstand online fire. Point in case, how many notifications do you think I have on this phone since we started talking?
DANICA	Err, two hundred /
RUCHI	Three thousand four hundred and twenty eight.
DANICA	Shut up.

She hands over the phone.

RUCHI	That's what we're withstanding. All self-righteous, all anonymous and all from people who can't spell.

DANICA   Grammar's not great either.

RUCHI   Nope, it's all totally 'an exempt table' or it's 'shooking' or a 'disk race.' See, that's another thing, about the man who said 'no press is bad press', and I assume it was a man in the same way I assume he was white and straight, he didn't have the burden of twitter.

She puts her phone away. DANICA's distracted from her job.

DANICA   Oh, so true! You know, I think a lot about when I was in Tibet/

RUCHI   Right /

DANICA   I was in this tiny town in the middle of the hills, and they had no internet service, at all, no matter how high you got. And I said to someone one day in a Starbucks: 'how do you cope?' She replied: 'as we always have, with each other.'

And I said, but what about Facebook? She didn't know; Twitter? No idea; Instagram? First time she'd heard it; Snapchat? Was like I was talking Chinese /

RUCHI   Mandarin's pretty big over there, I think.

DANICA   Yes, exactly, we don't need it. They avoid all that negativity and they live to, like, a hundred and five. It's literally killing us.

DANICA tends back to her posters. RUCHI's baffled.

Pause.

RUCHI   Well, exactly. We're on the same page.

DANICA   Yeah, it's you, me and some Tibetan people. Even if this situation is a little grey.

DANICA exits.

RUCHI   (*calling off*) Keep that to yourself.

DANICA   Huh?

RUCHI   Keep that - to yourself. We don't need mutiny in camp. Especially for someone who's only been here a month.

DANICA re-enters with a watering can, and begins watering the many pot plants. She blows the dust off some of the picture frames.

DANICA   No, nothing's changed, I'm still on Team Arthur Moses, now Olivier award-winning team Arthur Moses, I just think what he said last night was wrong, and he should have shown restraint.

RUCHI   Restraint is a word for civilians. Nothing our clients do is wrong, especially the profitable ones. In fact, exclusively the profitable ones. Their jokes are always funny, their work's invaluable and their discretions forgivable. That's our coat of arms and evening prayer rolled into one. You should say it before bed and after breakfast.

DANICA   I know that, but I /

RUCHI   There is no but /

The desk phone rings, with a different tune.

RUCHI/DANICA Client.

RUCHI   Go on.

DANICA moves to the phone. She then proceeds to practice a false, yet convincingly earnest, laugh. But soon stops herself, it wasn't high enough. RUCHI encourages higher.

DANICA   No, not.

She laughs again, it's higher and full of joy, like spring. **RUCHI** gives a thumbs up.

>   Got it.

RUCHI exits. DANICA answers the phone in a flash. Her persona is totally different on the phone, she's considerably more bouncy, and youthful and charming:

>   Is this the Olivier-award winning Arthur Moses?

She laughs the exact laugh just practiced and continues to throughout.

>   Yes, congratulations. Totally amazing. Totally.

>   No, supporting's the new leading. Trust me, same glory but without all that exhausting Day-Lewis shit. How's the head?

>   I heard, yeah, yeah. Was so funny, we're all still laughing 'bout it here.

>   Right, maybe not all.

>   No, she's not in yet, that's / she takes the tube, central line, deep underground, why you can't get through.

>   Of course she's not ignoring you, loves you too much. That's her trouble. Always has been.

Yeah, she's here. Let me just/ one second on hold.
Bye, darling.

She returns to herself.

    (*calling off stage*) Ruchi, it's Arthur, he'd like a
word.

A flash of a pause.

RUCHI   (*off stage*) Gimme a second.

DANICA   Just one moment, Arthur, there. She's coming.

She looks to check the coast is clear.

    For what it's worth, top tip, in Montenegro the
priests drink herbal tea with a raw egg upside
down to cure hangovers. Yeah. Just crack it
right in.

    They do it every day.

    Briefly, yeah, got back last month, was away
three years, yeah, yeah, all by myself.

RUCHI enters.

RUCHI   Tap me in.

*RUCHI storms over and the two tap each other's hands, like duel
wrestler's in a Smackdown Showdown tapping one another into the
fight.*

DANICA goes back to the phone.

DANICA   Ah, she's just here, Arthur, yeah, lovely talking,
bye darling. Bye bye. Bye. Yeah, bye. Great.

She hands over the phone.

22

RUCHI   Would you double count the number of interview requests, I think it's forty two.

DANICA agrees, silently, and exits. RUCHI speaks into the phone:

Ram? Good morn/ no, no, no, no, no, don't laugh, we're far from funny. Yeah. Long gone.

Yeah, really.

She flicks through the cuttings on the desk.

Of course, I have, and you feature - prominently. I'm waiting to hear back from Ofcom.

'Unprecedented' was the word she used, so that's something. Have you read the apology draft I sent you?

Why?

No/ you don't.

Really, Arthur, I / don't, not a good idea. No. We're on a time limit. I'm not going past ten on this.

Speed counts / no. Listen. Let me send it, sign it off. Please.

Stop. Stop.

She hangs up the phone.

(*to herself*) Fuck.

A moment with her thoughts, trying to calm.

(*calling out*) Danica! Dani!

DANICA enters.

DANICA   I got forty two as well, but we've had two more.

RUCHI   Arthur's on his way in.

DANICA   What? Why?

RUCHI   Feels he owes an apology in person.

DANICA   Oh, shit. The posters!

RUCHI   Leave the posters /

DANICA   No, I can't /

RUCHI   Leave the posters, I want you to take the statement on my desk and make it sound as if someone was saying it aloud. Punch it up.

DANICA   Aloud? / Why? /

RUCHI   We're doing a video apology.

DANICA   Are we? Is that /

RUCHI   Yes, quickly, go on!

DANICA turns and exits. RUCHI gets onto the client phone and dials a number.

RUCHI   (*on the phone*) Pick up, pick up, pick up, pick up, pick /

Voicemail. Visibly irritated.

     Ram. Pick up. This isn't the plan. You need to be absent, out of sight, not moving across London holding a bust of Larry Olivier's head eating a bacon wrap – what if you're spotted?

People think you're vegan for Christ's sake. Call me back.

She hangs up and looks to her phone.

        (*calling out*) Danica!

DANICA enters, holding the draft.

DANICA   I've had a look but I've forgotten how people speak.

RUCHI   Leave that a second, I need you to call Richard Santana.

DANICA puts the statement in her pocket.

DANICA   The guy from Metro 60 seconds?

RUCHI   He's just emailed, does he have a scheduled interview today?

DANICA   Err, yes, four o'clock / three, three o'clock.

RUCHI   What the fu / why did we give him an interview the day after the Olivier awards?

DANICA   We didn't think Arthur'd win and it'd be a good 'never mind onto the next one' piece.

RUCHI   We need to cancel it, Ram's ill clearly and publicly, he can't do it.

DANICA   Ram? Who's Ram?

RUCHI   Arthur, I mean Arthur. Sorry.

DANICA   Right.

DANICA goes to leave then returns.

What?!

RUCHI   Ramesh Ryatithih is known publicly as Arthur Moses because it sells a hell of a lot more tickets.

DANICA   'Kay. (*totally unsure*)

RUCHI   Arthur because it's British and kingly and Moses is just the right level of exotic. Now, go cancel his interview.

RUCHI goes to make another call. DANICA's still baffled.

DANICA   Right.

DANICA goes to leave then returns, again.

To be clear, I'm cancelling an interview for Arthur Moses with Richard Santana for today.

RUCHI   If you can muster the energy.

DANICA   And the other forty three?

RUCHI   Turn them down. He's doing none of them. This video's his only word.

DANICA exits. RUCHI dials a number on the phone. Voicemail again.

(*on the phone*) Ram, I'm losing patience and risked too much, you need to stop. Don't come in. She'll be here any second and if we're not tweeting something in an hour she'll /

ENTER DANICA. RUCHI hangs up the phone.

(*to DANICA*) That was quick, is it done?

DANICA   I've emailed him, but /

26

DANICA moves out the way of the door.

ENTER GRACELYN, holding multiple bags which she places on the chairs as she makes her way round to her desk. On her way, DANICA helps take her coat off her and stores it; RUCHI produces a cigarette and lighter, which GRACELYN accepts. Once at the desk, GRACELYN takes a moment to look at her computer and flick through the cuttings, all during...

GRACELYN So, there I was. Standing in the wings of the hall, I've been there twenty minutes, chatting with the sound techy, reassuringly dull, when that guy from that dolphin puppet show says into the microphone: 'best-supporting actor'. I was stunned, couldn't believe it. I'd be home before nine. Saved of all this toxic vanity.

She lights a cigarette and DANICA instinctively goes and shuts the door.

So, he's reading out the nominees, and I can see Arthur from where I am, spot his little face when his name's readout (he actually turned from person to person, checking they heard it too) and all I'm thinking about is whether South Ken is on the district or the Jubilee line? I'm beginning to favour the former when something occurs to me, something obvious but also hidden:

He's sitting dangerously close to the aisle.

And he's sat in the front row, amongst the proper actors?

And then... like a trance, or like a dream or like something else people who sleep have, dolphin man says...

27

The phone rings. GRACELYN answers.

You've really fucked a punchline for me, there.
Is it important?

She hands the cigarette over to DANICA, who quickly dabs it out and disposes of it outside the window. RUCHI then goes round to the desk drawer and procures perfume, which she liberally sprays around the room.

No. No. No, I'm not. No.

Well, it would go off, wouldn't it? It'd detect it.
The whole building would. Even in your
maintenance hovel.

I lit a candle. It's expensive. You wouldn't like
it.

I'll be vigilant. Right. Right, yes. Great. Bye.
Bye. Bye bye. Bye bye. Bye.

She hangs up the phone. She tries to remember where she was.

DANICA   What the dolphin puppet man said /

GRACELYN   What the dolphin puppet man said was: 'and the
               Olivier goes to: Arthur Moses. Long Day's
               Journey Into Night.'

She applauds quickly, then suddenly stops.

We all saw that production. All of us. We all saw
what he did at the Phoenix each night. It was a
performance which should've resulted in the
removal of his equity card, let alone an Olivier
award. But, apparently sense and taste have
evaded all of us, meanwhile he's charging to the

28

podium, bull-like, head first, and you can see there's something about him, in his stance, in his eyes, in the way he holds the award - he's pissed. He's completely pissed. And the rest, as they say/

DANICA   Is history?

GRACELYN   Is on the ten o'clock news. Two cunts, twelves fucks, three shits, and a partridge in a pear tree. And it's only Monday morning.

RUCHI   On the plus side.

GRACELYN   There isn't a plus side.

DANICA's phone buzzes.

DANICA   Excuse me. Richard, hi there, thanks so much for calling /

DANICA exits, her phone persona in full force. RUCHI moves round, showing the cuttings.

RUCHI   Here. Every one of these pictures of Arthur are of him on the red carpet. Even The Sun used a photo of him drunk from ten years ago, and they have photographers under the toilets. It's, pictorially, contained.

GRACELYN   I didn't let him do the winners press room. Charged him out of there like I was walking him to the gallows and stuck him in an Uber. Which I paid for!

RUCHI   Well, it's paid off. It's manageable.

GRACELYN   It's managing. Needs a little more to be done. Can I see a draft?

She gets out another cigarette and lights it.

RUCHI   We did write one then / I've had a change of heart about that.

GRACELYN   That doesn't sound good.

RUCHI   I've asked him to come in, I want to do a video apology.

A load fake laugh, which instantly stops.

GRACELYN   Ridiculous. Call him and cancel and tweet something. We have an hour.

The phone rings. GRACELYN answers.

        (*on the phone*) Have you got a bloody bloodhound in your office?

She hands the cigarette to RUCHI who disposes, sprays etc.

        Yes, I know it's not my greatest phrase, no, it does catch on the ear a little, it's the repetition; but, I can't always speak in gold dust, I have to reserve the shit for you.

She hangs up.

        Sorry.

RUCHI   I'm hoping for a ten o'clock post and I'm serious about the video.

A snap's pause.

GRACELYN   Why? Show your working.

RUCHI   I want to take him back to his roots, where we began, in YouTube videos. All of this is so far from who he is, I want us back on home turf, where people understand us and we're used to seeing him.

GRACELYN   This would be negotiable if we had a video, what we have is (I'm assuming) a hungover actor on a South West fucking train and a rushed script.

RUCHI   He'll be here on time/ soon, if that's your concern.

GRACELYN   It's entirely my concern, missing the sweet spot creates a growing vacuum of dark shit.

RUCHI   I know /

GRACELYN   The word out there gets nasty, news reports become unbiased and Piers Morgan starts having an opinion. Dark shit fills that vacuum and Arthur'll drown in it, we won't know we've missed it until it's too late.

RUCHI   He'll be here. Trust me.

GRACELYN   In the same way, trust me Arthur won't win and the Olivier's will be an easy night.

RUCHI   I didn't / I've apologised, I couldn't go /

GRACELYN shows her phone.

GRACELYN   Did you see Dickie's email?

RUCHI   I did and the day an agent leaves a profitable client is the day pig's fly.

GRACELYN   I think we should do the same. Cut Arthur loose too. Save him a train fare.

31

The room takes on a different atmosphere. It's tense and unsettled, and grows ever increasing.

RUCHI   (*v. softly*) What?

GRACELYN   I can't speak on behalf of someone I don't understand.

RUCHI   Understand? What does understanding have to do /

GRACELYN   I don't understand how someone can behave like that. Get so roaring drunk - if it was just alcohol – and say the things he said /

RUCHI   He /

GRACELYN   Attack the people that he did, friends of mine. If we cut our ties now I know we'd look good. We'd look – upstanding.

RUCHI   To the public, possibly upstanding; but, to the industry, other clients, what message does that send? We'll keep you, yes, when times are good, but when things turn south /

GRACELYN   Turn south? They've more than turned. We've changed direction, hit ice and are huddled amongst penguins.

RUCHI   Most of the young clients with us are friends, if one goes they'll all fly to another agency.

GRACELYN   Assuming they stick by him.

RUCHI   Yeah, 'cause it's the right thing to do.

GRACELYN   If I only ever did the right thing I wouldn't be standing here now, and neither would you, and nor would I have a tattoo of Dwayne Johnson on my thigh; I taught you better than to care for right. Don't assume it in others.

RUCHI   I don't like this sudden 'one mistake and you're out' policy. Who could survive that?

GRACELYN   Lots of people, and they now all work at Channel 5. Go and tweet something.

A slight pause.

RUCHI   You wouldn't be saying any of this if it was Felicity. Wouldn't cut her loose /

GRACELYN   How many Baftas does Arthur have? Cos Fliss has three /

RUCHI   If this was about her, you'd be on a plane to L.A. now, threatening the head of NBC with castration.

GRACELYN   Careful Ru.

RUCHI   Why is it different for Ram? Where's the line here? Cause from where I am, I'm struggling to see it.

GRACELYN   You forget, the reason he took this play was his search for credibility. Ha! I wouldn't trust him with my tea order, let alone another West End role.

The arrogance that he can snap his fingers and get his face on a poster. He embodies everything I hate in modern drama. Proves that you don't need experience, you need cheekbones. Followers are more important than training. The injustice of the casting room is found in him; all of them, popularity over talent.

I used to represent actors, and now I represent 'vloggers'. How the fuck did that happen?

RUCHI Because they are the future.

GRACELYN Only if we let them be. I'm up for grabbing marshmallows and watching Arthur burn out today. Might rekindle my love of the job.

RUCHI We'd burn with him. It's like that old adage 'publicists that scoff at progress and don't represent vloggers and youth, die.'

GRACELYN Who've you been reading?

ENTER DANICA, looking relieved.

DANICA I've been able to cancel/ sorry, should I?

She gestures to leave.

GRACELYN No, no, not at all. Come in, come in.

DANICA closes the door. GRACELYN sits down and begins looking through cuttings, more closely. She has a gift for doing multiple things at once: emails, writing and talking. She checks all constantly as we go on…

DANICA Santana is cancelled and I didn't need to offer anything in return.

RUCHI Excellent.

DANICA He understood, was there last night, and anticipated it wouldn't happen.

GRACELYN throws down a cutting.

GRACELYN   (*to herself*) Just rubbish, isn't it?

(*to DANICA*) Oh, Dani, Arthur's popping in, he wants to eek out our pain as long as possible, so if you wouldn't mind swapping the posters.

DANICA   Course, yeah.

DANICA begins rapidly taking down the pictures of JAMES and putting them in the cupboard and replacing them with pictures and posters of ARTHUR.

GRACELYN   Ru, have you got an actual time for Arthur or are we just feeling blind?

RUCHI   Not yet, but he's left/

GRACELYN   The second one. Fine. He's your client. If you miss it, you miss it. Any other news before we leave port into the shit storm?

DANICA   Kate is on her way to the shoot.

GRACELYN   Lovely, and the crew?

DANICA   Setting up in the ballroom as we speak. She'll arrive 4 minutes after they're set up.

RUCHI   Hair and makeup?

DANICA   Done in the studio. She said she'd send a picture.

GRACELYN   Perfect.

Holding a poster:

DANICA   Cannibal Fire, was that Arthur?

GRACELYN   Yeah, Cannibal Fire and that God awful prison
            and spider drama that was on at The National.

*DANICA continues with the poster. The phone rings.
GRACELYN looks who it is, and silences it by pulling out the
cord.*

            Channel 4.

RUCHI   I think Rory's phone interview went well too.

GRACELYN   How unlikely. They didn't ask about his affair?
            What are you giving instead?

RUCHI   I thought I'd trade them the news of Beth's
            twins.

GRACELYN   Oh, very good. It's a boy and girl.

GRACELYN sweeps all the cuttings across her desk into the bin.

            Okay, shall we start on Arthur, then? You done
            Dani?

DANICA   Yes, yes.

RUCHI and DANICA take a seat.

GRACELYN   Let's start with the vomit-stained cherry. I spoke
            with Official London Theatre on the way in and
            it goes without saying he's banned from every
            and all future Olivier awards ceremonies, and
            they want a full and public apology.

DANICA   Fair.

GRACELYN   More than fair.

RUCHI   We'll film the apology the moment he gets it here, and upload it before noon. The standard draft we started would work as a script, so he can use that as a prompt and /

GRACELYN   Where's that? I'd like to read it.

DANICA   Oh, it's, um / I have /

DANICA reaches into her back pocket and pulls out the paper and hands it to GRACELYN.

Here we are.

GRACELYN accepts the draft, and takes out a pen. She begins writing onto the paper, frantically.

GRACELYN   Ru, we'll handle this. Can you give Roxanne Reid a call, I've got thirty seven emails and seventeen missed calls. I think she wants my attention, so you can call her?

RUCHI   Okay. Remind me who she is?

GRACELYN   She's the head of Olivier broadcast and communications international and Social Media output. Me neither, feels like too many words.

RUCHI   I'll ask if there's an abbreviation.

RUCHI exits.

GRACELYN   Go easy. (*calling off stage*) (*to DANICA*) Okay, lets /

DANICA waits.

This is a good draft, Dani.

DANICA It was both /

GRACELYN Just some small additions.

GRACELYN continues writing for a beat, turning over the paper to continue her copious notes and then hands over the script.

> Here. Have him read that when-slash-if he gets here.

DANICA Great. That's / thank you.

GRACELYN finds the phone cord and tries to put it back into the phone. She does. It instantly rings. She checks the number.

GRACELYN Oh, for / it's fine.

She picks up the phone. DANICA stands and goes to leave, but as she does she begins to read the additions.

> Toby. How are you?

GRACELYN laughs – she uses the same phone voice as the others do.

> I'll bet, I'll bet. Well, know this, the only reason I'm picking up is because you're not going to ask me if you can interview Arthur Moses.

Pause.

> Go fuck yourself.

She puts the phone down.

> All alright?

DANICA Fine. Yes, yeah. Yea / you've added bits. Here.

GRACELYN Was I not allowed?

DANICA   Goodness, no, I didn't mean/ no, it just. Does it/ read wrong?

GRACELYN   Read wrong?

DANICA   These words, are they in the wrong order? Or, even, do they need to be there at all?

GRACELYN   Which words are we talking?

DANICA   You've added lots of 'we's' and 'ours'.

GRACELYN   More inclusive, yeah. All nominees together. One big happy, sweary family.

DANICA   Right, sure, okay, I get/ but this sentence, this, here, may I…? 'And I want to thank the Olivier sponsors, the champagne was just too good to ignore and I embarrassed myself with it.'

GRACELYN   Right.

DANICA   Is it right?

GRACELYN   Isn't it?

DANICA   It's not apologetic, it's excusatory.

GRACELYN   It's interpretable.

DANICA   As?

GRACELYN   The folly of youth, in this instance.

DANICA   Sure, but, should we not just apologise?

She finds it hilarious.

GRACELYN   'Just apologise', Just / I can't even say it with a straight face; no, no, no we don't do that honey,

39

no. Sit down for me, would you? 'Just apologise'.
That's sweet / so funny.

She does and GRACELYN recomposes.

This is your first, I don't know what you'd call it,
crisis management situation.

DANICA Yes.

GRACELYN Yeah, these need a different rhythm, these
moments. You'll have noticed that. It's not, I
don't know, trivial, confirming Rory's affair or
Kate's tax avoidance. This matters, Arthur
embarrassed the British Theatre industry to the
rest of the world. Has Ruchi told you about the
sweet spot?

DANICA Yeah, she explained.

GRACELYN Good, when we say is just as important as what
we say.

Absolutely, we need to say sorry. We need to
speak about what he did, because what he did
was wrong. It was indefensible.

DANICA Yes, I couldn't /

GRACELYN That being said, we shouldn't leave him out in
the cold. We should protect him. And that line,
'the champagne was just too good to ignore', it's
relatable. We try and cut a few of them into
things like this.

Hearing Arthur Moses embarrassingly admit he
gets drunk and makes bad choices in the Royal
Albert Hall connects him to Steve who gets

drunk and makes bad choices in Basildon; and it's that connection which will make his apology accepted. He's not an out of touch, talentless, lucky twat, he's a young boy who couldn't resist free alcohol. That's it. We've all been there.

DANICA   I don't drink.

GRACELYN   Give it time.

It's sentences like that which demystify. You never think of Brad Pitt taking a shit, do you? Do you?

But he does. Everyday. Twice on Tuesdays. Think of that now. Think of the image. Him sitting down and depositing yesterday's food. Sometimes it takes two minutes, sometimes twenty, either way there's always sweetcorn in it, why? Because everybody does it. And even remembering that happens makes you like him just a little bit more. Steve from Basildon remembered that. And that's why he went to see Ocean's 12. Liking someone translates into buying their product.

DANICA   Yeah, I can understand that. I did economics at A-Level and almost got a B. But, Arthur won't be speaking a relatable, 'human' line here, he's shifting the blame/

GRACELYN   We don't talk blame at this stage /

DANICA   The champagne wasn't too good to ignore and the incident was avoidable; 'cause if it wasn't everyone would've got drunk and slurred their speeches. And the fact they didn't means that we saw the biggest miracle since Jesus' Oscar-winning performance feeding the five thousand.

GRACELYN   Jesus didn't win the Oscar.

DANICA   What?

GRACELYN   It went to Judas, it's a meatier role. Lots of monologues and inner conflict.

DANICA   I stand corrected.

She makes the sign of the crucifix:

GRACELYN   I bless and forgive you.

DANICA   Shouldn't we just say he's wrong and he's sorry and he won't do it again? Isn't that the moral thing to do?

GRACELYN   Moral?

DANICA   You know, I think a lot about when I was in Bolivia /

GRACELYN   Right /

DANICA   I was lying in my hostel, reading an old Time Out, when a young man came running in, all flustered and scared and nervous. His name was Alberto, he told me he was in a lot of trouble, that he'd stolen from someone who'd turned about to be quite the prominent drug lord and he didn't know what to do. I calmed him down and explained to him that honesty is always the best policy in these matters.

GRACELYN   He ran into the wrong room /

DANICA   And after a little persuasion and a cup of tea, he agreed. He went to the Lord's Den and explained everything and he just apologised. Plain and simple. And you know what? Everyone respected him.

GRACELYN stands and makes her way to her window. A small picture, one of the few none 'work' photos on the side, catches her eye. An old boxing photo.

GRACELYN   What happened after that?

DANICA   I don't know, I wasn't in the compound. But, I can only assume they're now the best of friends. And that's my point.

GRACELYN   What point? One's a drug lord and the other's almost certainly dead, what point were you making?

A pause of confusion. She scrambles for something.

DANICA   Morals are important/

GRACELYN   Alright /

DANICA   I got a little lost, but that's my point. That's the thing to know.

GRACELYN   Look at this.

She throws the boxing picture to her.

DANICA   Is that you?

GRACELYN   I used to box; my father did, and his father did, so I did. Proper fighters we were. Bloody buggers.

There's a moment in every fight, shared fighter to fighter, where one's been defeated, lost in their spirit and strength, but it's yet to be called.

You're all but fighting a dead-woman. Do you finish it and let them fall or hit harder for ever daring to step in? End or create pain? That's a moral question.

But this, all of this, this is candy floss. It's a game we play. It's putting words in the right order. There's no real loss, morality doesn't enter this ring.

DANICA Why did you quit boxing?

GRACELYN I didn't quit, I left. Knowing when to leave is as much of a virtue as soldiering on.

DANICA Why leave then? If it was so good?

GRACELYN 'Cause there comes a point in every adult's life where you have to stop punching and start using your words, so PR felt the obvious move. It's where the new world battles are. Lucifer won't ascend in a flaming chariot, he'll be smuggled in a press release. It's how the world'll end: under embargo.

GRACELYN lights a cigarette.

Your trouble is the company you keep. Two high-court Catholic lawyers, it's not good on the soul. Don't get me wrong, I adore my sister; but, you've spent too long on the side of the angels. You can breathe now. De-clench.

DANICA smiles.

> Welcome. Don't fight it. The show always goes
> on.

A phone rings, but it's muffled.

> I definitely unplugged it.

*She goes over to her phone to double check: it's unplugged. They
both quieten to listen to where it's coming from. It's the cupboard.
They go to it and open it. GRACELYN pulls out a ringing phone
piece. She answers.*

> (*on the phone*) Hello?!

> I was NOT smoking.

> How did you even get it fucking in there, it's a
> locked cupboard. Stop hiding phones in my
> office?

> (to **DANICA**) Change the locks.

DANICA exits.

> You've crossed a line, Phil. A clear line.
> Apologise all you want, I / dare you! Come up,
> here. See what happens.

She slams the phone down.

> (*to herself*) I mean. How? I can't.

*She pulls the phone out of the cupboard. Questions what to do with
it and then throws it out the window. She makes her way back round
to her desk and plugs her own phone back in. It instantly rings.*

45

She picks it up, and immediately hangs up. She then takes the piece of paper with the apology on it and a pen and reads it through, again.

She seems to write and change certain parts. ENTER RUCHI.

GRACELYN How's Reidy?

RUCHI Roxanne Reid has the longest job title and shortest grip on reality.

GRACELYN Doesn't she just?

RUCHI She's insane, that woman. And rude. What she wants, what she's asking for – well / demanding for – is an apology.

GRACELYN Right.

RUCHI But, she wants grovelling, begging. Hands and knees. Game of Thrones 'shame' levels of apology.

GRACELYN I thought you wanted to stick by him? Isn't giving them what they want and making it go away doing that?

RUCHI The only reason she wants all this is because people keep tweeting at her and she's scared. She's saying we must heed to the 'tone of the nation' - aside from online White Knights, no-one really gives a shit, no-one's hurt, who even listens to the Olivier awards! Half the population think you've misspelt Oliver and the other half don't know what you're talking about.

GRACELYN It's example setting /

RUCHI	And I'm not calling online parents liars, but how many children were listening to Radio 4 on a Sunday night? Really? How many are 'corrupted permanently' or 'scarred for life'? They're just words. It's all self-inflicted significance.
GRACELYN	Alright, what are we really talking on this? Is she exaggerating or is it bad?
RUCHI	It's – not ideal, it's unpleasant. I can feel we're running out of time.
GRACELYN	So tweet something then. Finish it. Or I will.
RUCHI	No, that's what she wants. That's just what she wants. 'Where's your statement? Where's your statement?'

RUCHI references one of the posters with Arthur's face clearly on it.

Why should he grovel to her? This man. How dare she demand he get on hand and knee. Others have done far worse and she's stayed silent. No, not having it. Where's the draft now?

GRACELYN takes the piece of paper from the desk and hands it to RUCHI who begins reading.

GRACELYN	Ru, back in the day, I used to box Roxanne Reid – don't repeat that. Not very often, but it happened. She was a terrible boxer, much in the same way she is a person now; but, one thing she never did was back down. She's like a cockroach. You can punch her in the head as many times as you want, she'll get back up, she'll be cross eyed, but she will do it.

47

DANICA enters and takes a seat.

RUCHI Which is why we're bringing a gun to this knife fight and using a weapon Roxanne Reid doesn't have and can't imagine: The Fandom.

GRACELYN The what?

RUCHI We're going to use Arthur's fans and their blind faith towards him against her.

DANICA Is this in the apology?

RUCHI Yeah, we're going to target the apology directly to them. Not even acknowledge the angry illiterate twitter people. We're going back home, and talking to the countless fans who've already forgiven us, who don't think we've done anything wrong. If you've got enough total, young loyalty you're unstoppable. And we do.

Look at this

Reading the statement.

sorry, sorry, sorry, sorry – four times.

GRACELYN Alright /

RUCHI He's not a paedophile, he's not a racist / rapist / murderer, they don't apologise four times, why would he?

She tears up the written apology.

DANICA That was mainly written by you.

RUCHI Even if we did apologise four times people wouldn't accept it. They see / hear / know what they want to. Always have. The world is a personal experience, you build it all yourself.

GRACELYN An earnest apology ends the event. It's something corporations can point to as a mark of returned faith.

RUCHI The faith didn't go anywhere, what left was indifference. Normal, everyday people care now.

DANICA They're angry, sure /

GRACELYN He'll lose the clothing deals and the public appearances and future projects. I've seen this happen.

RUCHI No he won't, a million seventeen year olds tweet him every day. Every single day. Countless times. I know this, I read their messages, I reply to them. He's still got the power to make money, that's not gone, and that's always sexy.

GRACELYN And for those who don't find him sexy?

RUCHI I can get them back on side too. I know I can.

GRACELYN How?

Pause.

RUCHI I'm not sure yet

GRACELYN scoffs.

But I'll figure it out. I will. We'll do a Q&A or something, he can donate money to a charity. Those living with swear scarring. I don't know yet, but fans are the key. That's certain.

GRACELYN   Can I be honest with you now, Ruchi? I don't care what happens to Arthur in this cross fire; genuinely, couldn't give a shit, swim or drown. But if we're fighting, and Roxanne Reid's involved, I don't lose to her. Ever.

RUCHI   We won't. In seven years, from your Office Runner, bringing you tea, to where I am now, when have I ever disappointed?

Short pause.

DANICA   This reminds me of my time in Kuala Lumpur/

GRACELYN   Oh, for /

RUCHI   Timing, Dani, really /

GRACELYN   Please /

DANICA   Let me say it, let me, context is everything, hear me out, you need to know this,

Something alights in RUCHI.

I was walking down this dirt track road when I saw a young Sherpa /

RUCHI   Say that again.

DANICA   Young Sherpa?

RUCHI   The first bit.

DANICA   Dirt track?

RUCHI   No, the first bit!

DANICA   One hundred and twelve missed calls?

RUCHI	About context / something /
DANICA	Context is everything?
RUCHI	Yes!
DANICA	Well, context is everything, it's why you need to know Fernando the Sherpa had a wheat allergy.
RUCHI	Context. There it is. Context. That's what the twitter people don't have. They don't have personal context, they don't know him. They just have the result or what they've read or heard or guessed at.
GRACELYN	So?
RUCHI	So, that's how we tell the apology, as a story! Like the ones you bloody tell.
DANICA	Me? /
GRACELYN	Go on.
RUCHI	We let him tell them what happened. From the person who did it. Let his personality seep in. We direct it to the fans but speak to the others. Anyone / everyone will get it.
DANICA	Making it relatable? That's needed.
RUCHI	Exactly, yes, relatable. We tell the whole, long completely honest story, starting at the beginning, unlike we've done before, working to the end with one apology, making it feel natural; and Roxanne Reid can fuck off with her 'hands and knees'!

GRACELYN   Oh, very good. Very good. One 'sorry', Reid won't like that at all, will you Reidy?

GRACELYN punches the speedball in her office with incredible force.

DANICA   Hang on, just one apology? Is / is that enough?

GRACELYN   Yes, it'll make her sweat / boil in anger. She'll want ten, just one is perfect.

DANICA   But, does it appease the online masses, though?/

RUCHI   Yes? Tell me yes?

GRACELYN   Yes, we're doing it! Dani, go and get the board from under your desk.

DANICA exits.

GRACELYN   Time check. When's Arthur here?

Checking her phone.

RUCHI   Arriving at Paddington in fifteen, then getting an Uber.

GRACELYN   No underground!

RUCHI   I've said no underground, he wouldn't /

GRACELYN pulls down a cord at the back of her office, which reveals a large charred sign reading: 'brave', 'inspiration', 'honest', 'sorry' and 'good character'.

Christ, that's still there.

GRACELYN   Hello, old friend.

RUCHI   I thought we lost that in the fire?

GRACELYN   No, always there, written in holy rock.

DANICA re-enters with the board and sets it up.

DANICA   What's that?

GRACELYN   The speech writer's gospel. The five points we need to hit repeatedly throughout for mass impact.

DANICA   Good character?

RUCHI   Means, like, 'upstanding'?

DANICA   Oh, right. And brave? Inspirational?

Noticing the board set up.

GRACELYN   Ah, good. Ru, over to you. Dani, at the mark. Who starts it?

DANICA grabs a board marker and stands read to write. GRACELYN takes a seat. Pause, slight unease.

RUCHI   Right, well, good stories start at the beginning. Danica, you tell the same stories as Arthur did in his early videos, how would you start it?

DANICA   Uhm. Well, 'hello' is always a good start.

She goes to write but stops when…

GRACELYN   No! Definitely no, we're not starting with hello.

DANICA   Not hello?

GRACELYN   Guilty people start with hello. Strangers, criminals, politicians start with it.

DANICA   Is it that it's formal?

GRACELYN It's too formal and it's too prepared.

RUCHI We need natural, to friends. What about 'hi?'

DANICA I like hi.

GRACELYN Yes, it's casual, part of character – 'hi'

DANICA writes it.

They throw the word back and forth to each other, like friends playing tennis in summer. This continues for as long as is possible and funny:

RUCHI (*curiously*) Hi?

GRACELYN (*casually*) Hi.

DANICA (*trying to convince herself*) Hi?

GRACELYN (*sternly*) Hi.

RUCHI (*she doesn't like it*) Hi?

DANICA (*cruelly*) Hi.

And so on, until:

RUCHI (*solemnly*) Wait. I've got it.

Hey.

GRACELYN Oh my. (*taken aback*)

DANICA Holy shit.

GRACELYN Write that down!

DANICA does.

RUCHI Said in the right way.

GRACELYN   Said in that way.

RUCHI   'Hey' can be honest, sorry and characterful.

DANICA   Hey it is. 'Hey', 'hey'; then I'd probably be like, Hey – guys /

GRACELYN   Too masculine.

DANICA   Hey girls.

GRACELYN   Too feminine.

DANICA   Hey everyone.

GRACELYN   Too many.

DANICA   Should someone else write this?

RUCHI   Let's make it inclusive now, and specific; talk to the fans; create a 'them' and 'us'. I think he used to call them his 'Mo-team' originally. Let's say 'Hey Mo-Team.'

DANICA writes this.

DANICA   'Hey Mo-Team', you know what might be quite nice is if he asks after them; 'hey Mo-Team, how are you all?'

RUCHI   Very nice / but he'd say 'you all good?'

She amends and writes.

DANICA   Cool, like he's worried about them/ they're his concern in all this.

GRACELYN   It's good character too!

DANICA	'Hey Mo-Team, you all good? Hope so. I'm -' How is he? Is he upset?
RUCHI	He's more than upset.
GRACELYN	Devastated?
RUCHI	He's less than devastated. Maybe he's 'here'. 'I'm here.' Present in the moment, but also in the video and consoling.
DANICA	Alright /
RUCHI	Make a dash, though, we need a pause after 'I'm', he'll have to sell it.

She does this.

GRACELYN	We should acknowledge the lateness, this should've been earlier.
RUCHI	Okay /
GRACELYN	Use the one 'sorry' to set the tone.
DANICA	'Sorry for my lateness I/ couldn't get to you'?
GRACELYN	Too weak an out.
RUCHI	Couldn't find the words?
GRACELYN	Still too weak – 'Sorry for my lateness' – oh, write this – 'sorry for my lateness, I just needed time to reflect'

DANICA does.

DANICA	Oh, nice, I'm saying that from now/
RUCHI	Excellent word /

DANICA   Can't make it to Nandos tonight, girls, I need time to reflect.

GRACELYN   Good, isn't it? When my father left he gave me this beautiful letter explaining everything. It was perfectly crafted, every word mattered. Said no more than he needed to. And it concluded with: 'I just need time to reflect'. Used it ever since, it's perfect here.

DANICA and RUCHI don't know what to say.

DANICA   That's – lovely /

RUCHI   Yeah.

DANICA   I think, maybe.

GRACELYN   Yes.

RUCHI   Let's reference why we're here / why it's happening. What if: 'Listen, about last night'?

GRACELYN   It's a bit one-night stand-y. 'About last night'. Sounds like it's said with a coffee the next morning.

DANICA   It's rarely coffee, tends to be Listerine.

GRACELYN   No harm in saying 'yesterday's Oliviers', is there?

RUCHI   Fine/

DANICA writes:

DANICA   'Listen, about yesterday's Oliviers' /

RUCHI   Now, we're going to do 'not the real me'. Like we did with Rory on that affair rumour.

GRACELYN English, Ruchi.

RUCHI We're going to divide him in two. Separate the him that acts from the him that he is, cause if we can do that, we're unstoppable. Nothing'll ever stick to him.

DANICA Oh, yeah, I've used that on a few boys. 'Of course I'd have called you back before now, that's the real me. You know that.' In fact, this one time in Mozambique /

RUCHI No, no time. Let's make it personal, to them, 'Listen, about yesterday's Oliviers, you know me' /

DANICA 'You know about me, about who I am' /

RUCHI 'What I am' /

DANICA 'What I do' /

RUCHI He inhales, pausing, distancing himself, he thinks, he speaks: 'Yesterday wasn't the real me. That was' /

DANICA 'Someone I don't recognise. Someone I don't like and who I try not to be, someone I hide, it's' – no I've lost it, had it and lost it, I'm not sure about that.

GRACELYN Unsure of what? This is diamond dust. I don't know what either of you are talking about, but I know I like you! You're both telling me about the distant 'real you' – which is bullshit, everyone is always the real them - but the way you say it –

it makes me want to help you become the 'real you'.

DANICA   Seriously?

GRACELYN   This is 'inspirational', I'm inspired, it's like I dreamed a dream.

RUCHI   Had a dream, dreamed a dream is Les Mis.

GRACELYN   Whatever, it's working and he'll sell it. Dani, finish the thought. Someone I hide it's –

DANICA   Uhm, 'it's the /' what is it? 'it's / the side of myself that I hate'.

GRACELYN   Lovely, nice bit of self-loathing in there. Self-loathing's all five, is it all five? Yeah, it is. Very brave. We've said so little with so much, it's exactly what we need.

RUCHI   I can't tell if you're joking or not?

GRACELYN   I haven't told a joke since 1992, but this is very good.

RUCHI   When I wanted this before you pushed back on every turn. Said it was juvenile / silly, you said.

GRACELYN   That was different, Rory was and is having an affair. The real him was inside a French actor.

RUCHI   But the 'real him' wasn't. The 'real him' was at home drinking tea and watching Andrew Marr. This is my / it's the greatest PR contraction since 'sorry'. It ticks all of your five and fifty more. How does it not keep you up at night?

Anyone can say it and anyone can mean it, it's been democratised, everyone can claim the difference because it feels true. Everyone has genuine, somehow, believable distance from their actions.

We've condemned and lynched Hyde, while kissing Jekyll. No-one can do anything wrong, because no-one did anything wrong. This phrase directs anger at shadows.

Best part – from our view, for Arthur and his teen fans – is that if you don't know the real me, then you know 'the real me'. And that's the one people believe because it's the one they want to believe.

Trust me, we'll be using it, I'd say, daily in a few months, for everyone. Dani, let's start our story, 'side of me that I hate' what would we say next?

DANICA   Yeah, hate, uhm, / probably / 'and I wanna tell you what happened', that's what I'd say, get my word in first /

RUCHI   Yes, like everyone else is wrong or lying /

GRACELYN   Hang on, hold/ staying on the 'real me', do they know about his anxiety? I can't remember.

RUCHI   His anxiety?

GRACELYN   Arthur's fans, do they know about his catastrophising?

RUCHI   I'm sure he tweets about it.

Looking for confirmation.

DANICA	He's mentioned it in interviews too. I can find a cutting if /
GRACELYN	No, no, fine, it's just - mental health's in vogue now, we could mention it?
RUCHI	Vogue?
GRACELYN	Nobody'll listen to you nowadays if you've got all your shit together.
DANICA	So true, I'm fucked. I wouldn't follow anyone who wasn't.
GRACELYN	Is he seeing anyone?
RUCHI	Romantically?
GRACELYN	Medically – why would I care romantically? – for his anxiety.
RUCHI	Dr. Finch, seen him for years /
GRACELYN	Great /
RUCHI	Started when he was seventeen, I think /
GRACELYN	So we can say he's getting help?
RUCHI	If you think it'll add to it?
DANICA	I always quite like it when celebs talk about that stuff, when they're open and real with you. You feel less, I don't know, alone.
GRACELYN	Exactly, might come in handy. And 'getting help' is a good personal decision. It's a 'get out of jail free' card, it's self-conviction. To declare it.

RUCHI   Alright, it's in the back pocket if we find a moment.

Returning to the apology.

'I wanna' tell you what happened' /

DANICA   Yeah, 'tell you what happened' /

RUCHI   Maybe we do another inclusive bit again? 'Tell you what happened away from everything? /

DANICA   'Away from all the cameras and the lights'?

RUCHI   Yeah, like it, it's good, shelter him /

DANICA writes.

GRACELYN   Another thought, maybe just me, is anxiety enough?

His anxiety, I mean is that enough? Do we think? It's just / well, Danica, your mum was telling me about your anxiety.

DANICA   Yeah.

GRACELYN   What type is that? Like Arthur's?

Struggling to say the word, for effect:

Catastrophising.

RUCHI   (*confirming*) Catastrophising.

DANICA   Uhm, I don't really know the type, it's just since coming back from travelling and having that panic that I don't know what I'm doing, or everyone is ahead of me or better, I'm lesser somehow, I won't /

GRACELYN   See, that's anxiety /

DANICA   Okay.

GRACELYN   I don't really know what it is, but it's that, it's such an umbrella, it's a hundred things, but depression I understand. Depression is crystal clear and singular. Maybe we should change it to depression for Arthur? He's got depression. People get depression they don't get anxiety.

DANICA   People get depression and anxiety.

GRACELYN   No, not get as in get, get as in 'I get that'. Depression's worth more, you know? In the mental health cash point. The man on the street gets it.

DANICA   Well, maybe, but Arthur suffers /

GRACELYN   What do you think Ru? Will this beat Roxanne Reid and save Ram? I think it will. She doesn't have this.

RUCHI   I / I don't know /

GRACELYN   Sorry, what's the time again? Can't read the wall with my eyes.

RUCHI checks her watch.

RUCHI   9:45.

GRACELYN   Thank you, what were you were saying?

Taking a second.

RUCHI   I think depression will be a good way into the main story /

GRACELYN   Great, I agree, now he's depressed. Wonderful. It's so many more brownie points. Plus, it's the 'real him' from the real him.

DANICA   I'm not so sure /

RUCHI   It's all five, and connects the intro to the narrative, can do it that way /

DANICA   Maybe we should check with Arthur first? It's his own health. He might not feel comfortable /

Beyond sweetly:

GRACELYN   Darling, darling, from now on, Arthur speaks how we write he speaks. Last night proved he can't pick his own words, so we do it for him. It's what he pays us for.

DANICA nods.

RUCHI   In the beginning, can we change 'here' to 'coping'.

DANICA amends.

I also want to hype up your thought Dani, Arthur's opinion being the only valid source.

DANICA   Right.

RUCHI   'Tell you what happened and show you my' – my what, what's he showing? The one person who knows what happened.

GRACELYN   Eyes?

RUCHI's unsold.

RUCHI   Reality? My reality, maybe?

GRACELYN   Life? Day! 'Show you my day'.

DANICA   Truth. That's what all this is, technically, it's his truth.

DANICA writes:

'Tell you what happened and show you my truth'.

GRACELYN laughs. RUCHI loves it.

GRACELYN   Oh, 'My truth', it's untouchable.

RUCHI   It's honest, brave, characterful/

GRACELYN   It's outrageous. Roxanne, you hear that? Ya fucked. I thought 'the real me' was good, but this – people'll use this in court. You've just free'd criminals. Absolutes are absolutely out now. Then what? Plough into his depression?

RUCHI   Yes, immediately. Start at the top / just write key words here, Dani, Arthur can link them.

DANICA writes:

Begin in the beginning, woke up and he was feeling /

GRACELYN   Depressed!

RUCHI   Exactly. So he didn't eat. Empty stomach. Good. What did he do all day?

GRACELYN   Cry!

DANICA   No /

RUCHI	No, he didn't cry, he stayed in bed. Arthur stayed in bed and watched the clock / thought about the night ahead. He ignored calls, didn't want to talk to anyone / let's get some pity.
DANICA	Do we /
RUCHI	Then he had to get dressed, let's say his suit didn't quite fit right, keep him grounded. Hair, teeth, mouthwash, slight stain in the corner, boring everyday things.
GRACELYN	He's just like me!
RUCHI	Getting there, how did he get there?
DANICA	He got a black Mercedes /
RUCHI	No, he didn't, he got public transport. Underground. Cheap. Off peak. Arrivals / did you do the carpet?
GRACELYN	No, we would have had to queued for eight miles and meet youths. Two things I don't do for anyone.
RUCHI	Ah, no-one'll know. I loved seeing you on the carpet, 'you give me strength' – write that, 'you give me strength'
GRACELYN	The youths will know we're lying /
RUCHI	They'll just assume they missed him. Weren't there early enough, or were looking elsewhere. There were pictures of him on it.
GRACELYN	By the step and repeat at the top.

RUCHI   All leading, all leading, all leading to: the free
                 alcohol,   depression,   drinking,   cocktails,
                 photographs, crowds, shouting, scared and
                 nervous and 'probably had more than I should
                 have' /

GRACELYN   'Probably' – amazing /

RUCHI   Surprised I won / ashamed myself when speaking
                 / I'm getting some help for it / hope for
                 forgiveness / we'll beat it together / I need you
                 more than you need me and I love you /

GRACELYN   Oh /

RUCHI   'I love you'. End on 'I love you'.

*RUCHI sits, delighted, DANICA still writing. GRACELYN's
delighted, claps a little.*

GRACELYN   He's a very lucky man.

RUCHI   They all are.

GRACELYN   Where is he now? Must be close.

RUCHI   I'll look.

RUCHI checks her phone.

GRACELYN   D'you get all that, Dani?

DANICA nods.

DANICA   Think so, yeah. Key bits.

RUCHI   Reid's emailed me /

GRACELYN   Ignore her. Will you type that up for us? So it's
                 manageable, nice big font for him?

DANICA   Sure.

GRACELYN   Pleased that's sorted, I've got other clients to pander to today, meeting George at the Savoy for eleven, then Rory's gala tonight. Christ knows why I agreed.

RUCHI   She's just written 'BBC One Now' with a smiley face emoji and a dagger.

DANICA   That doesn't sound good.

RUCHI goes over to the television and turns it up. On the television, a reporter sits at a news desk.

REPORTER   ...confirming at least seven dead within the area and twelve in varying critical conditions in hospital. More on this ongoing story as it develops.

In entertainment news, the actor Arthur Moses stunned audiences at the 2019 Olivier Awards last night by his use of excessive profanity during its live broadcast. Moses, known originally for his YouTube career, won best supporting actor in a play for his performance in Long Day's Journey Into Night.

The speech is plagued by loud bursts of laughs from the audience, which diminish as he goes on.

BLEEP. *I mean,* BLEEP*ing hell, this is* BLEEP*ing mad. Yeah,* BLEEP. BLEEP. *Right, please and thank yous, like mum says, y'alright mum? We* BLEEP*ing won!*

Yeah, God, there's a lot of you, um, right, start at the top. Dickie, my agent, you're a complete BLEEP, *but I love you, man – What? He is!*

Arthur Moses, there. Roxanne Reid who is the Head of Olivier broadcast-

DANICA   Oh my God.

REPORTER   and communications international and Social Media Output.

GRACELYN   She gave a quote.

REPORTER   Has issued the following statement on behalf of the BBC and Official London Theatre:

The below rolls on screen.

> *'All of us here at the BBC and Official London Theatre are shocked and appalled by the language used by Arthur Moses last night. It was profanity which we deem totally and wholly unacceptable for any broadcast, let alone a live show pre-watershed.*
>
> *We wholeheartedly apologise to all those listening and to those who were offended by Arthur Moses' language. And wish to convey our own bemusement and upset that Moses, and his team, seem unrepentant in his silence.*
>
> *An investigation will begin immediately into what further steps need be taken in regard to this breach of broadcasting law and any future involvement between Moses, SOLT and the BBC.'*

RUCHI   We've missed it. We're too late.

GRACELYN   Yeah.

REPORTER   At time of receiving that statement, Arthur Moses was yet to comment on any of the events last night.

RUCHI   'Was'?

REPORTER   Until twelve minutes ago. When this selfie emerged on Twitter showing Arthur Moses on the Jubilee line hugging two tourists.

The image is shown on screen. GRACELYN exits, punching the speedball on the way. RUCHI goes to the client phone and dials a number.

Moses has his Olivier award between his teeth and appears to be wearing the same tuxedo from the night before. The caption reads: #Moses #SummerLondon #whathappenedlastnight?

RUCHI   Fuck SAKE! (*to the phone*) Call me back and get off the underground and head here, please Ram!

RUCHI slams the phone down. DANICA looking to a phone.

DANICA   Twitter's exploding. The picture's had two thousand retweets.

ENTER GRACELYN, turning off the television and holding a large bundle of notes.

RUCHI   Grace, I told him, I said no underground/

She tries to show her phone, GRACELYN bats it away.

Look, I said / look, there /

GRACELYN   I'm sure you did, Ru. I'm sure, because you respect this building. You respect what I've built since I was twenty-nine, what years of work and endeavour have created here, my reputation, you understand how fragile this all is. How impossible it is for credibility to return once lost. You understand all that, don't you?

RUCHI   I'm sorry.

DANICA   What do we do now?

GRACELYN   Ruchi?

That question's to her. Tell us, your client, you waited, what do we do?

Struggling to think:

RUCHI   I / have no idea. I don't know.

GRACELYN   I do.

We obliterate them, Danica.

She places the folder onto the desk.

SOLT, the BBC, his critics, tweeters, we categorically, unequivocally fucking obliterate them. We shift from defence to attack; reaction to provocation. We bring an atom bomb to this knife fight and we end it now.

In this folder, lies every BBC rule and regulation still in existence. Everything. From how much the BBC Director General is allowed to earn to how little detergent must be used in the men's toilets in Wogan House. And since 2008 I have

71

been working my way through and finding flaws in the wording, saving clients embarrassment, and worse, in the process.

DANICA   How did you /

GRACELYN   They are a public organisation and I am the public.

RUCHI   How do we use it?

GRACELYN   The right question. What we have written so far is strong, that can stay; but the apology needs a new ending, one which returns fire; strongly but subtly.

RUCHI   And it's in there?

GRACELYN sifts through finding the appropriate page.

GRACELYN   Somewhere, yes. We're looking for a loophole to exploit. Specifically (I think) in section five, category: harm and offence, subsection: Live Broadcast; sub-subsection harm and offence in a live broadcast.

See, the wise owls at the BBC say that language is only deemed offensive in its context. If Scarface swears everyone's happy, if Peppa Pig does it's a problem.

She moves to the board, passing DANICA the notes on the way, and begins drawing a mind map, with Arthur's name at the centre on the easel.

There are ten rules – Dani, as you'll see - to which live context is measured, and we need to find the constitutional failing that happened last night and speak it aloud.

RUCHI What failing?

GRACELYN Exactly, I don't know yet. But one did. One did or we're creating one that did, then we're throwing it back.

RUCHI Amazing.

RUCHI finds a notepad and paper.

DANICA Is this lawful?

GRACELYN Probably. Usually. Generally. I don't know, let's see what we find. We're up against the wall now. Strap in, girls. Let me show you how bendy guilt can be. Read us out the first one.

GRACELYN is poised to write. DANICA, taking a moment:

DANICA Editorial Guidelines. Section Five. Regulations determining the extent of harm and offence within live BBC broadcasts. Regulation One: The time at which the content is available.

GRACELYN Ah, not obviously helpful/

RUCHI 7.30 programme began, he spoke about ten to eight.

GRACELYN Primetime.

RUCHI Pre-Watershed too.

GRACELYN writes 'primetime' and 'watershed'.

DANICA Everybody heard it.

GRACELYN   Not necessarily a bad thing.

RUCHI   Really?

GRACELYN   Even in the most watertight, regulations there's something we can take forward to the next. In this case, it's that it was heard by the biggest audience of the night.

RUCHI   Okay.

DANICA   Old and young, that's a good thing?

GRACELYN   It is what it is. Gimme the next one.

DANICA   Regulation two: The service on which the content was / is available. So, Radio 4.

GRACELYN   Well, shit. What's that coming over the hill, is it a monster? No, it's the middle-aged and they're pissed.

She writes 'Radio 4'.

RUCHI   His language goes against their whole identity as a radio station.

DANICA   It does feel worse given Songs of Praise was on before and repeated afterwards.

RUCHI   Like they were trying to cleanse themselves.

GRACELYN   The problem with Radio 4 listeners isn't that we're middle aged, it's that we write into things. We complain, and we care – and whether the opinion be good or bad, we say it.

RUCHI   We were at 10,700 complaints at last check this morning.

GRACELYN Right /

DANICA Do people still write into things?

GRACELYN writes down '10,000'

RUCHI Though, Ofcom said, at some point, they'll stop counting and just pick a gasp-inducing number.

DANICA You've circled 'service' here, Grace. Does radio make a difference? The 'service', radio, is that maybe less offensive than television?

GRACELYN Yes, Dani, very good, very - good. Doesn't spread as wide.

She writes down 'radio > TV'.

DANICA No gifs, that'll do it.

GRACELYN I don't know what that is, but yes.

RUCHI I'm wondering too, we don't see his face, that's also a good thing. It's not attached to him saying it. There's division.

GRACELYN Yes, yes, good. We're on a roll, what's the next one?

DANICA Regulation three: Surrounding broadcasting content.

GRACELYN writes down 'Surrounding'

GRACELYN Yeah, yeah, I know this. 'Surrounding', that word is the keystone, so our focus is either side of the incident. I've used this one before. Got a client absolved from a lifetime ban by arguing that the surrounding pre-show adverts were more sexual than the live show's 'wardrobe malfunction' – a phrase I coined, incidentally. Everyone uses that now. Dani's right context is everything. Last night, who won before Arthur?

DANICA   Errr, I'll double check.

DANICA gets out her phone and Googles.

RUCHI   How'd you manage that? How'd you even start to argue it?

GRACELYN   Well, the context of such a sexually explicit laundry ad before the accident diminished the impact of the slip, or so I said then. It prepared the audience, implied a certain 'raunchy' level.

           Plus, I was so fierce in the fight, didn't budge an inch, crushed 'em. I even got, and this is scout's honour truth, even got the director general to say the phrase 'what's a left nipple among friends' as he apologised.

RUCHI   Amazing.

GRACELYN   Easier times.

DANICA   Sadiq Mansari won, costume design. Fourth award of the night.

GRACELYN writes down 'Mansari'

GRACELYN   And did Mansari say anything provocative in his speech?

DANICA   Not remotely, called for equality in the workplace.

GRACELYN   Boring fucking liberal.

She scrawls through 'Mansari'.

> Who spoke before Mansari? After Arthur won't
> make a difference.

She consults the computer.

DANICA   Rachel Rickwith-Smith: choreography, how far
back do you want to go on this? The start, or/

GRACELYN   Basically, did anyone other than our pony
attract any negative attention?

DANICA   No, no-one. Everyone else said nice things.
Equality, unity, transparency and Cameron
Macintosh, those were the themes of the evening.

GRACELYN   Fine. So we're taking forward that he was
entirely the point of focus. Next, what's next?

DANICA   Regulation four: the extent to which the nature
of the content can be brought to the attention of
the potential audience.

She stops writing, looks around. Almost laughing.

GRACELYN   Oh, hello; it's like music, that one, say it again
for me.

DANICA   The extent to which the nature of the content
can be brought to the attention of the potential
audience.

GRACELYN   You feel that? That fizz? That 'here we go'
sensation. It's in this regulation, girls.

*GRACELYN flips the chart and writes down, in large writing,
'nature of content', 'extent to which' and 'attention of audience'. Her*

excitement palpable. DANICA looks to RUCHI for clarification, but is met with bafflement.

DANICA   You've highlighted quite a lot in this one, there's/

GRACELYN   I know what there is, I've highlighted 'extent to which', and 'nature of the content' and 'attention of the audience'. They jump out at you, don't they? Can't avoid them. This meeting of one size fits all and pained specificity. Now, we just need to find which of these can be – well, PR'd.

DANICA   PR'd?

GRACELYN   Yeah, we're gonna PR the shit out of it!

One of these wasn't done properly. One was our constitutional, unequivocal and appalling failure. Let's start with 'Nature of the Content'. Here / bored of writing…

They swap pen for notes, and DANICA makes her way to the board.

…someone else's turn. 'Nature of the content', then. What would we say, friendly? Jovial? What was the nature?

DANICA   'Friendly'?

GRACELYN   Yeah.

DANICA   I'm not sure it was 'friendly'.

RUCHI   It was, he didn't say it the way it sounded /

DANICA   What does that mean?

RUCHI   It was meant warmly. He'd naturally say that to people. Dickie is / was a friend.

DANICA   He calls his 'friends' /

GRACELYN   (*leaping in*) Yes we all know what he called him, but you have to remember Dani, Arthur is from the East. Have to bear that in mind. Write down 'eastern'. Maybe add 'lawless.'

DANICA does.

RUCHI   My point is that the problem was the setting, not the word.

GRACELYN   Yes, because the word itself, from Arthur, was silly and friendly.

RUCHI   Right, and so was the nature.

GRACELYN   Sure, write down 'silly' and then 'friendly'.

DANICA does.

               No, write down 'drunken silliness'. More appropriate.

She amends.

               And make a note, I like what you said Ruchi, at some point in the speech, to mention Arthur's 'nature' or him being 'natural' or him 'naturally', something with that core. That root. It's good, links back to 'human' and 'youth' and that can get us into 'cheeky'.

DANICA writes again.

Now 'extent to which...'. 'Extent' is an interesting word, it's the BBC giving themselves a loophole.

With a word like 'extent' you can go as big or small as you want; but, it gives us a loophole too, because no matter the extent, you never go far enough.

RUCHI Sure.

GRACELYN What extent was it made clear it was a live show?

RUCHI Very clear.

DANICA Definitely before the broadcast and repeatedly throughout.

GRACELYN Good. That's good. People know things go wrong in live shows.

DANICA Clearly.

GRACELYN So we can use that. It's a live show, things go wrong, people say what they don't mean, it's tense, it's stressful in live shows, it's scary. Make a note that we need to include that it was live in the speech.

DANICA does.

What other extents happened after?

RUCHI Of the words? Or the offence, maybe?

DANICA Not that I could hear. It was pandemonium, took five minutes just to wrangle the laughing.

RUCHI   Maybe it's the BBC's apology – they apologised immediately after the show, didn't they?

DANICA   Yeah, did a standard 'Sorry for any offence caused.' And gave a number to ring if you were affected.

GRACELYN   No, nothing's strong enough. Let's move on, move on to the last one. Attention of the audience.

RUCHI   Well / know it was primetime, biggest audience.

DANICA   And he was the focus of the night, only controversial part.

RUCHI   Everyone was looking at him, centre of stage.

DANICA   And he was uninterrupted during the speech/

Something ignites GRACELYN.

GRACELYN   Uninterrupted?

Yes, he was, wasn't he?

She delves into her notes.

DANICA   Yeah.

RUCHI   Does that mean something?

GRACELYN found something, she can barely contain her smile.

GRACELYN   I've always liked you Danica. You know that? Even when I didn't know it, I knew it.

DANICA   Why?

The phone rings, a client's ring.

ALL   Client.

DANICA checks the phone.

DANICA   Arthur.

RUCHI   Let me.

GRACELYN Dani come with me. We need to check something. The game's afoot.

GRACELYN exits.

DANICA   Help me.

DANICA follows. RUCHI makes her way to the phone, composes herself before answering.

RUCHI   (*on the phone*) Ram? No, no, no / listen, I said / yes, listen to me,

I said don't do it. I said come straight here! Do you have any idea how much it's cost to keep you? How much I'm at risk / we look like idiots!

He's right to drop you, I don't blame him. They're all right too. You're an anchor, pulling us down.

I don't know. I'm trying, desperately, but I don't know, if she says go there's nothing I can do. I've tried.

Yeah. Straight here. Now. Yes? Now. Good.

And Ram? We've come such a long way. In two years, such - we need to make this work, is what I'm trying to say. You and I. Alright.

She hangs up the phone and takes a moment to think, then moves to the board and has a look through the notes.

Soon GRACELYN enters, with purpose, and an apple – mid eating and not really listening, followed by a sheepish DANICA.

GRACELYN   Is he far?

RUCHI   Dickie's left him. Sent him a text.

DANICA   A text?

RUCHI   Dickie, Public Management and he lost Adidas, they're all running a mile /

DANICA   I'm sorry.

GRACELYN takes the pen and writes 'Charlie Piper' on the board.

GRACELYN   So? Is he walking or on the tube? 'Cause if he's still on the tube /

RUCHI   He's in a car leaving Baker Street. He thinks he's going to lose everything.

RUCHI notices the board.

GRACELYN   And he would – if he didn't know me.

GRACELYN'S finished writing.

RUCHI   Who's Charlie Piper?

GRACELYN   A question we should have asked ourselves a long time ago. He's our guardian angel.

RUCHI   Our what?

GRACELYN Yeah, I don't believe in any of that crap either, but that's what he is – a big, fat, juicy angel. He's Jesus on toast.

DANICA makes her way to a chair and sits slowly.

RUCHI Why's that then?

GRACELYN 'Cause of his job. He's worked with Cannibal Fire (*she points to the poster*) but, more importantly, on last night's Olivier ceremony – he's in the live sound department. He monitored the quality of the audio.

RUCHI I don't follow.

GRACELYN To misquote Hugh Grant: 'blame actually is all around'.

It's his fault. This man. This BBC sound man, the chaos of last night.

He should have cut Arthur's microphone the moment he stood on stage. He should have silenced the broadcast after the first 'fuck' and he should have changed transmission to The Archers after the third.

There was a constitutional, unequivocal failing on the part of the BBC. The extent to which the nature of the content was shown to the largest possible audience was permitted by their failing. They let it happen!

The very public whom they need and protect were made vulnerable to this profanity because of them.

Because they weren't doing their job.

It's selfish to assume it's only him at fault, and selfless of us to remind that to others.

We have found our loophole, girls; and what's better, it's a genuine flaw in the system. We are right. Not had to make anything up. It's him to thank for the fact Arthur spoke for an uninterrupted minute and seven seconds.

Tell me Ru, how much d'ya you love me?

RUCHI   You said he's sound quality.

GRACELYN Him? Yeah.

RUCHI   What you're talking about is censoring, that's producer's work, he wouldn't have been involved in what was broadcast.

GRACELYN It's all the same world. It's all in the 'noise' category.

RUCHI   Not really. A sparrow couldn't do the work of a jump jet, but they're both in the 'flying' category.

GRACELYN Person on the street doesn't know that. 'Sound department' I mean, who cares? It's just a list of names at the end, normally someone's talking over it.

RUCHI   Sure, but the failing's on the producers. He doesn't /

GRACELYN Yeah, Arthur doesn't know any of the producers.

RUCHI   Okay.

GRACELYN   That's the thing. That's the / what we're trying to avoid here. This guy's the key. They know each other.

RUCHI   How?

GRACELYN   Dani?

DANICA   He did the sound on a Cannibal Fire music video. One of the ones Arthur was in a few years back.

RUCHI   Right. And?

GRACELYN   And it's important to say now/

RUCHI   We're going to blame him? Let's call it for what it is, Grace, we're gonna' blame him? This man, who had as much to do with last night as we did, we're blaming him?

GRACELYN   We're not blaming anyone. I wish we were in a position to blame people.

DANICA   She calls it 'nudging'.

GRACELYN   We're gonna' nudge 'em.

DANICA   Blaming in any other voice.

GRACELYN   When did you become so literal? Ignore her. This entire position, which Arthur created has /

RUCHI   No, I told him to come in. It was me.

GRACELYN   We both know you didn't, and we'll come back to lying later, 'cause we have something else now. Something which'll prove he's earned that award.

RUCHI   What?

A brief pained pause.

GRACELYN   I want Arthur to nudge this man in his apology. I want him to fake a friendship based on that music video and playfully joke that he should have cut him off last night and spared him all this.

                      It'll plant the seed of shared guilt. Given everything, it's as close to an attack as we can muster, we can't be seen to be retaliating. Played naturally and earnestly and charmingly we'll get away with it.

RUCHI   We'd name him?

GRACELYN   Briefly.

RUCHI   We'd put his name in it? In the video?

GRACELYN   Yes.

RUCHI   Wh – I mean, fuck, Grace.

GRACELYN   Yeah.

RUCHI   No, really: fuck.

GRACELYN   What do you want me to say? I know it's ugly, but it's everything you wanted.

RUCHI   Say there's an alternative.

GRACELYN   There isn't, and this is solid – and magnificent if I'm honest with you. I've surpassed myself.

DANICA   But, it's not true.

GRACELYN   It's better than true, it's believable.

RUCHI   Throwing his name into this mix, it's already
            going to be a bonfire and mentioning him in it /

DANICA   He'll never work again /

RUCHI   Never. Publicly named by Arthur Moses over
            this /

DANICA   We're calling him incompetent, this sort of thing
            lasts /

GRACELYN   What are you basing this on? Your years of
            hiring sounds technicians?

DANICA   That you're going to unleash fifteen million fans,
            charging towards him, all furious that he let
            Arthur go through this.

GRACELYN   Is that a touch dramatic?

DANICA   We're addressing everything to the fans, what is
            that if not a battle cry?

GRACELYN   He'll be fine, his publicist will write some clever
            response.

DANICA   He's a bloody sound technician, he doesn't have
            a publicist.

GRACELYN   Don't be ridiculous, the world is made of
            publicists: those who have them and those who
            are them. No-one else exists.

RUCHI   Come on, Grace /

GRACELYN   I'm being glib / the BBC will give him one if
            needed, but it won't be.

RUCHI	Well /
GRACELYN	You're both acting like we're killing him, anything we do will be done nicely. Arthur must remain the good guy. It's a nudge, is all.
DANICA	Good guy?
GRACELYN	Yes, and if not 'good' then equally bad/ he's not all to blame.
DANICA	He's the one who swore.
GRACELYN	But the microphone projected it.
DANICA	He deserves better.
GRACELYN	So do I!
RUCHI	Alright, let's just think /
DANICA	I can't / I'm sorry, I stood by on his mental health, cause, maybe, I don't know / but I – I won't on this. We can't do it / shouldn't name him. Sorry, Grace. No.
GRACELYN	What do you think, Ru?
RUCHI	It's a horrendous idea.
DANICA	Thank you.
RUCHI	But, we've still got to do it, obviously. There's no question, we've got to. Ram has to be saved, Dani. I can't / can't not.
DANICA	What?

RUCHI checks her phone.

RUCHI   I have to. Come on, we've got six minutes. Let's just write something and end all this and make it go away.

GRACELYN   Yes.

RUCHI tries to get to the board to write.

DANICA   'Have to'?

RUCHI   Yes. Where do we start / a 'wish' maybe? He wishes, something /

DANICA finds it almost amusing:

DANICA   Oh, I didn't see it. How could / how've I missed that one? Normally so on it. Course, you 'have to' Ruchi. You 'have to', don't you? 'Cause you're the biggest fan of all. You're sleeping with him.

RUCHI   No, Danica, I'm not.

DANICA   That's the real you. Shagging the clients, all this gung-ho, you're sleeping with him /

RUCHI   No /

DANICA   What else prompts such blind loyalty?

GRACELYN   Ruchi is that /

RUCHI   My loyalty, Danica, is based on that people like us, like me and Ram, don't come back from this. It's hard to get in the room, and it's even harder for us to stay there. This industry doesn't give us second chances. It latches onto our mistakes and bites down. Everything's so much / so much greyer than your stories. I'll be damned if he leaves when I'm here to fight his corner. My loyalty is unwavering but it's far from blind.

Now we need to write this speech, and we need to nudge Charlie Piper; and unless you have a real story about condemning innocence, may I suggest you go to the door and help get Arthur in quietly and undetected.

DANICA stares for a moment, looking between them and exits.

Pause.

Sorry, I know she's your niece / or something, isn't she? /

GRACELYN No, no. You have the stomach of PR, she has the stomach of a Carebear. Bound to clash. Can't imagine she's here for long.

RUCHI How do we do this, then?

GRACELYN As a guillotine would.

GRACELYN moves over, RUCHI hands over the pen. She scans the page, getting to the end of the speech. She writes:

'It's funny to think that my friend' – Charlie, isn't it? /

RUCHI Yeah /

GRACELYN 'Charlie, in the sound team, could have cut off my microphone when I spoke. Stopping what I'd said and protected the listeners.'

She takes a step back.

He wouldn't care if the listeners are protected / fans, he would, but not the listeners.

RUCHI   No.

GRACELYN   It's too formal too. Maybe, just, 'Charlie, and the sound team'? Can deflect a bit off him too? And do we get to it quick enough? Is it too short?

RUCHI   Needs stronger, where's your grit?

RUCHI takes the pen from GRACELYN and begins writing the below:

> '...cut off my microphone when I spoke. I wish my old friend Charlie, who was there last night, could've helped me out. Cut my sound off or something, I don't know, saving all this.
>
> He's a friend who knows my mental struggles and when I started to say what I said I wish he'd saved me from myself. Hidden the 'me' I try to hide. I am my own greatest enemy, and I only wish there were more out there to help me in my fight.'
>
> What do we think?

GRACELYN checks her watch and lights a cigarette. RUCHI stares at the speech.

GRACELYN   Time of death: 10.17am. I've never liked the BBC anyway. Are you happy with it?

RUCHI stares at the speech. DANICA knocks on the door, poking her head in.

DANICA   He's here / waiting outside.

GRACELYN begins dabbing out the cigarette, rapidly.

GRACELYN   Fuck it.

DANICA motions how close he is, and GRACELYN shifts as per her false phone manner, very loudly:

> Ah, excellent. How wonderful and so soon! That's just great, isn't it great? God, I'm happy! Let me come say hello. Where is he? Come on, where is he?

The lights start to fade down (except the neon sign) as GRACELYN moves to the door to say hello. RUCHI continues to stare. GRACELYN and DANICA exit.

> (*off stage*)   Darling! You must've had the most appalling night – ah, Darling! You look so tired / oh, don't mention it, don't mention / long as you're alright.

The television then flickers on. Arthur is sitting in a white shirt, hair ruffled.

He sits for a moment, then begins, becoming gradually more emotional as he speaks:

ARTHUR   Hey, Mo-Team.

> You all good? Yeah? I hope so.

> I'm just – coping at the moment, you know? Second by second. Breathe in and then back out.

> Sorry for my silence on this – I, just, needed time to reflect by myself, you know? There's been a lot of / you've probably seen.

You guys know me. You know about me, about who I am, what I do – yesterday, at the awards, that wasn't the real me, obviously. That was someone that I don't like, don't want to recognise – it's someone I don't want to be. I hate myself that you saw it.

It's not right.

But, I want to tell you what happened and I want to do it away from all the lights and cameras and people that don't really know me, and wanna hurt me, haters / journalists. I want to say what my truth is.

To you.

He recomposes.

I, naturally, woke up feeling really depressed and I was tense about the evening ahead. My stomach was all in knots, so I wasn't eating or anything or drinking, really, was just taking it step by step.

Like, once I (eventually) got outta bed, it was time to get ready so I got changed into my old suit – it was my school one, it was so tight. I did my hair, brushed my teeth and mouthwash – the burning kind – and I took the tube to the Royal Albert Hall, district, south Kennington, and it's just so mad there. I was so nervous. So many people. But, I love seeing you all and chatting with you – you genuinely gave me strength for it. Really.

I went in quick, though, cause of everything. Felt a bit, like, drowned. I'm getting help with it all now, but I still need to self-manage it. So, thought I'd duck out – and then they were giving away this free champagne.

It was this, like, weight of my illness which meant I took more champagne than I probably should have – I was suddenly really thirsty and hungry, it kinda caught up on me – it's something I don't normally do and am really embarrassed by and it led to what happened.

I'm sorry if people were offended by the words I said at that moment, I'm ashamed of what I said on live radio. I think lots felt I shouldn't have said them, and I do too.

I just keep going over it in my head. Naturally, I feel sick when I think on it.

Just wish my old friend Charlie, who was there last night, could've helped me out. Cut my sound off or something, I don't know, saving all this.

He's a friend who knows my mental struggles and when I started to say what I said I wish he'd saved me from myself. Hidden the 'me' I try to hide. I am my own greatest enemy, and I only wish there were more out there to help me in my fight.

Thinking today it's a fight so many of us are on, so many of us are struggling and getting through it and we will beat. Even when it hits us hard and makes us do things we don't like, we can beat it. We will, together. We'll beat it.

I pray I can get past this, and you'll help me.

Remember that I love you. And, I need you so much more than you need me. Catch you soon.

Pause.

Arthur then bursts out of character, he's a cocky, arrogant and self-assured and speaks to someone left of camera.

Boom! Nailed it! That felt good, how'd it look Ru?

RUCHI   (*Off Screen*) Good. Great.

ARTHUR   Good? Yeah. I've got another one in me, I can cry sooner or maybe a bit more? Just give me a second. Need some more eye drops, though. It feels so fucking good. They're gonna' love it.

RUCHI   (*off screen*) No, we need to post this. We got it, we got it.

ARTHUR   Yeah? We got it. That's great. So great. Oh, it's good to be back!

He laughs, as he does the television switches off.

The neon light flickers and then turns off.

The End.